W9-DEL-083

MAY 2017

SandCastle

Rhyme Time

The Rare Fair

Pam Scheunemann

Consulting Editor, Diane Craig, M.A./Reading Specialist

ABDO
Publishing Company

Published by ABDO Publishing Company, 4940 Viking Drive, Edina, Minnesota 55435.

Printed in the United States.

Credits
Edited by: Pam Price
Curriculum Coordinator: Nancy Tuminelly
Cover and Interior Design and Production: Mighty Media
Photo and Illustration Credits: BananaStock Ltd., Brand X Pictures, Corbis Images, Hemera, Image 100, ImageState, Tracy Kompelien, PhotoDisc, Stockbyte, Thinkstock

Library of Congress Cataloging-in-Publication Data

Scheunemann, Pam, 1955-
    The rare fair / Pam Scheunemann.
        p. cm. -- (Rhyme time)
    Includes index.
    ISBN 1-59197-814-9 (hardcover)
    ISBN 1-59197-920-X (paperback)
    1. English language--Rhyme--Juvenile literature. I. Title. II. Rhyme time (ABDO Publishing Company)

PE1517.S45 2004
428.1'3--dc22
                                                                        2004050432

SandCastle™ books are created by a professional team of educators, reading specialists, and content developers around five essential components that include phonemic awareness, phonics, vocabulary, text comprehension, and fluency. All books are written, reviewed, and leveled for guided reading, early intervention reading, and Accelerated Reader® programs and designed for use in shared, guided, and independent reading and writing activities to support a balanced approach to literacy instruction.

Let Us Know

After reading the book, SandCastle would like you to tell us your stories about reading. What is your favorite page? Was there something hard that you needed help with? Share the ups and downs of learning to read. We want to hear from you! To get posted on the ABDO Publishing Company Web site, send us e-mail at:

sandcastle@abdopub.com

SandCastle Level: Transitional

Words that rhyme do
not have to be spelled the
same. These words rhyme
with each other:

chair

rare

square

dare

hair

stair

mare

stare

pair

tear

Savannah is sitting in the dentist's chair.

Katelyn told Zoe, "I **dare** you to swing as high as me!"

Tamara and Hana both have curly hair.

Mia, Amanda, and Jordan will take turns riding the **mare**.

Juan is shopping for a new pair of shoes.

Colin likes his burgers to be
well done, not rare.

Mark sits next to his dad on the stair.

Riley looks through the **square**.

Clara is careful not to tear the flower petals.

Owen was so surprised at what he saw on the computer that all he could do was **stare**.

The Rare Fair

* Welcome *

Blair dreamed of a fair.
There were crazy things everywhere.

She saw an elephant in midair.
It was wearing yellow underwear.

Blair saw a parrot
eat a pear
while standing
on a snare.

Then a tiger
rode by in a chair
that was being pulled
by a grey mare.

And she couldn't
help but stare
at the very rare unicorn
with bright pink hair.

Then she saw
a fortune-teller named Cher
with some dancing silverware.

Before she awoke,
Blair heard Cher declare,
"Don't despair!

The next time you dream,
the rare fair will still be there."

Rhyming Riddle

What do you call two matching blocks?

Square pair

Glossary

mare. a female horse

rare. meat that is lightly cooked so it is still red in the middle; excellent and extraordinary

snare. short for snare drum, a double-headed drum with strings or wires on the bottom that rattle when the drum is played

stare. to look wide-eyed at something for a long time without looking away

unicorn. an imaginary animal that looks like a horse with one horn growing out of its forehead

About SandCastle™

A professional team of educators, reading specialists, and content developers created the SandCastle™ series to support young readers as they develop reading skills and strategies and increase their general knowledge. The SandCastle™ series has four levels that correspond to early literacy development in young children. The levels are provided to help teachers and parents select the appropriate books for young readers.

Emerging Readers
(no flags)

Beginning Readers
(1 flag)

Transitional Readers
(2 flags)

Fluent Readers
(3 flags)

These levels are meant only as a guide. All levels are subject to change.

ABDO
Publishing Company

To see a complete list of SandCastle™ books and other nonfiction titles from ABDO Publishing Company, visit www.abdopub.com or contact us at:
4940 Viking Drive, Edina, Minnesota 55435 • 1-800-800-1312 • fax: 1-952-831-1632